NEW

SALFORD SENTENCE READING TEST

MANUAL

New *SSRT*

NEW
SALFORD SENTENCE READING TEST

MANUAL

G. E. Bookbinder
Revised and restandardised by
Colin McCarty and Marie Lallaway

HODDER
EDUCATION
AN HACHETTE UK COMPANY

Acknowledgements

Our thanks go to Wakefield Learning Support Service advisers Diana Sutton, Olivia Jones, Julie Banks and Adele Hornsby, who gave much valuable advice, which helped ensure the three forms A, B and C were comparable. Special thanks go to Debbie Mole and the children of St Luke's Primary School, Tiptree, and the children and staff of Redcastle Furze Primary School, Thetford, who participated in a number of the development trials. Finally, our thanks are due to Catch Up and all the pupils and staff at the schools listed at the end of this manual, who took part in the final standardisation trials.

The development of the new sentences was undertaken by Marie Lallaway, who devised a sound and helpful way to review the previous Salford sentences and create new, up-to-date material. We then refined the sentences to be closely matched across the three forms. Colin McCarty developed the comprehension questions, and trialled the various iterations of sentences and comprehension questions to produce the final version, which we hope will allow teachers to explore whether the pupil has *understood* what he or she has decoded.

The detailed independent statistical analyses were undertaken by Tony Kiek to provide secure and reliable standardised scores and reading ages, together with statistical data to confirm these data.

recommended by

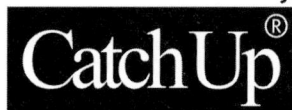

CatchUp®

www.catchup.org

Catch Up is a not-for-profit charity which aims to address the problem of underachievement that has its roots in literacy and numeracy difficulties.

Orders: please contact Bookpoint Ltd, 130 Milton Park, Abingdon, Oxon OX14 4SB. Telephone: (44) 01235 827827. Fax: (44) 01235 400401. Lines are open 9.00–5.00, Monday to Saturday, with a 24-hour message answering service. Visit our website at www.hoddereducation.co.uk

First published in 2012 by Hodder Education, an Hachette UK company, 338 Euston Road, London NW1 3BH

Impression number 6 5 4 3
Year 2016 2015 2014 2013 2012

Printed in England by Hobbs the Printers Ltd, Totton, Hampshire SO40 3WX.

A catalogue record for this title is available from the British Library

ISBN 978 1 444 14944 9

CONTENTS

INTRODUCTION   **5**
    Developing the new test   6

ADMINISTERING THE TEST   **8**
    Preparation   8
    Test conditions   8
    Giving the test   8
    If you also want to assess reading comprehension   9
    Assessing progress   10

SCORING AND INTERPRETATION   **11**

DEVELOPMENT AND STANDARDISATION   **17**
    The 2011 standardisation   17
    Reading and comprehension ages   18
    Reliability and validity   18
    Standardisation and norms   19

STANDARDISED SCORES   **22**
    TABLE A: Reading accuracy for ages 5:6–11:3   22
    TABLE B: Reading accuracy for less able readers aged 11:4–13:0   28
    TABLE C: Comprehension for ages 5:10–12:7   30
    TABLE D: Comprehension for less able readers aged 12:8–14:0   34

READING FOR MEANING interpretation graph *(photocopy master)*   **37**

Quick Guide

⬇

Decide upon starting sentence.

⬇

Inform the pupil how to do the decoding test, and whether you will be asking the comprehension questions after each sentence.

⬇

Begin reading and continue to the sentence in which the 6th error is made.

⬇

Record each error by circling it on the Record Sheet, or add miscue information.

⬇

Note comprehension performance, literal and inferential.

⬇

Note number of 6th word error, and record Reading Age.

⬇

Transfer information to front of Record Sheet.

⬇

Refer to tables for comprehension age and standardised scores.

INTRODUCTION

The *New Salford Sentence Reading Test* is a brand new version of the *Salford Sentence Reading Test* first published in 1976, which was developed by Geoffrey Bookbinder, then head of the Reading Advisory Service in the metropolitan borough of Salford.

The original test consisted of three equivalent forms (A, B and C), each containing a series of 13 oral reading sentences of graded difficulty, designed to provide a quick, economical and accurate measure of mechanical reading ability up to the age of 10 years 6 months. The test appealed to teachers for its simplicity of administration and scoring.

The *New Salford Sentence Reading Test* preserves and extends these characteristics:

Original features

- three equivalent, or parallel, forms;
- quick and economical test delivery;
- rapid and simple scoring system;
- assessed mechanical reading ability, or reading accuracy (decoding text);
- gave reading ages and percentiles.

New features

- four additional sentences per form, to improve discrimination and assessment reliability at both ends of the reading ability scale;
- a wider range of reading ages;
- two questions (one literal and one inferential) accompany every sentence, providing an optional measure of comprehension, including comprehension age;
- gives standardised scores as well as reading and comprehension ages, and percentiles.

Additionally

- the context of each sentence reflects experiences which are appropriate to pupils at the relevant age;
- all sentences use language in a wholly literal sense, so making reading accessible for pupils who have English as their second language and/or who may not have grown up in Britain;
- scoring uses only 'counted' words that are not repeated across the sentences.

The *New Salford Sentence Reading Test* provides both reading and comprehension ages and standardised scores based upon a sample of over

9000 pupils taking 18000 tests. It is suitable for screening a pupil's reading ability by:

- quickly obtaining a reading accuracy age or standardised score;
- obtaining a comprehension age;
- comparing reading accuracy to comprehension.

This can be achieved in a one-to-one session of 4–5 minutes per pupil.

Developing the new test

In undertaking the revision we adopted a systematic strategy.

First, each original sentence was reviewed using the following criteria:

- grading the decodability of each word;
- analysing the structure of the sentence;
- determining the formality and familiarity of the vocabulary;
- reviewing the context of the sentence for age-appropriate conceptual understanding.

In the light of this analysis, existing sentences were kept, modified or replaced.

As well as modifying many of the original sentences, twelve new sentences were written to add two new easier and two new harder sentences to each test form:

- two 'basic' sentences to make reading ages below 6 more reliable and the tests more useful for younger children or poor readers – by improving discrimination in the 5–7 reading age range;
- two 'challenging' sentences, in terms of syntax and vocabulary, to make the test more useful for pupils in Years 5 and 6 and in secondary schools, and to allow good progress to be measured.

The *New Salford Sentence Reading Test* thus has 17 sentences in each of the three forms A, B and C, and the three forms have themselves been carefully balanced to be equivalent in demand.

In addition, to allow teachers to measure **reading for meaning** (comprehension), as well as reading accuracy, two questions were written to accompany each sentence. One question focuses on investigating literal meaning, the other on the ability to draw inferences from what has been read.

The *New Salford Sentence Reading Test* remains true to the intentions of the original test, therefore, but places it firmly within a contemporary context.

The recommended use of the test is from chronological age 6. Although reading ages are given from 4:5, these are intended to provide discrimination and give insight into the reading difficulties of older, less able pupils rather than to represent the typical performance of children much below the age of 6.

The test is suitable for use by classroom teachers and teaching assistants wishing to *individually* assess individuals or groups of pupils in a relatively short time – for example, to form a broad impression of the range of abilities in a new class at the beginning of a school year. The three parallel forms mean that the test is ideal for use before and after an intervention strategy, to monitor progress.

Although the main strength and merit of the *Salford* is that it provides a semi-formal and normative aid to classroom assessment by teachers, it is also capable of acting as a larger-scale screening test, on a school-wide basis, or as part of an initial assessment for use with pupils with suspected reading or learning difficulties.

With up-to-date norms for both reading accuracy and comprehension now available as standardised scores, the test may also be used for Access Arrangements testing at Key Stage 2.

ADMINISTERING THE TEST

Preparation

You will need a copy of the Record Sheet as well as this manual. The pupil will need one of the reading test cards (Form A, B or C) from which to read the test sentences. If you are seeking to assess a pupil's reading comprehension as well as reading accuracy, you will also need to refer to the Comprehension Test questions provided on the separate cards.

Test conditions

It is important that the pupil first reads the sentences without discussion, collaboration or help, although your manner should be generally encouraging and reassuring. After each sentence, you may ask the two comprehension questions, **provided the pupil has made no more than two reading errors in the sentence or you have not supplied more than one word to maintain reading.**

Giving the test

The pupil can begin at any point on the test at which he or she is able to read two consecutive sentences without any errors. In practice, younger pupils and those in the early stages of reading will start at the beginning, but more confident and fluent readers may start at a later sentence. If the pupil is unable to read two consecutive sentences without errors at the point at which he or she began the test, you should re-start the test at an earlier sentence, where they can be completely successful on two sentences, before continuing up the sentences.

Experience from trialling suggests the following places are convenient to start for *average* readers.

Year	Sentence number
1	1
2	5
3	7
4	9
5	11
6	12
7 and above	13

If in doubt, start the test at the beginning. Testing typically takes four to five minutes per pupil, often less.

Testing stops when the pupil has completed the sentence in which the **sixth** error is made. Mark the pupil's errors on the Record Sheet by ringing each word in bold type that is read incorrectly, or use suitable miscue analysis markings if you wish to gather more detailed information. **Note that *only* the words in bold type are counted for scoring purposes.** Do not make any marks on the non-bolded words – these are usually simpler (or repeated) words which are required to maintain sense but which are not of the same demand as the counting part of the sentence.

If a pupil is unable to read as far as the first word for which a reading age is shown on the Record Sheet, scoring is not possible: the reader has not reached a level for which a meaningful reading age could be estimated. In this case, an appropriate note or comment may be entered on the Record Sheet and an alternative, more appropriate assessment used, such as the *Phonics and Early Reading Assessment (PERA)* for younger pupils.

As a matter of good practice, you may wish to encourage the pupil to continue to the end of the sentence on which the sixth error is made, or read the remainder of the sentence with him or her. However, this is not essential for the purposes of the test.

If a pupil reads a word incorrectly, but spontaneously corrects the mistake, it is not counted as an error. When a pupil is unable to produce a word after 6 seconds, supply the word and record it as an error.

A suggested wording for you to use when introducing the test to the pupil is:

'I would like you to read some sentences for me. They are quite easy at first, but each one gets a little harder. If some of them get too hard, I will tell you the words.'

If you also want to assess reading comprehension

A suggested wording is:

'After you have read a sentence, I will ask you two questions about it. Use the information in the sentence to help you make your answer.'

'This is an example:

*The sentence is: **Tom was drawing in his book.***

Question 1: What was Tom doing? The answer is: drawing.

Question 2: What do you think is in Tom's book? The answer could be: pictures or drawings, not pages or writing.'

You do not need to keep to this verbatim – the most important thing is that the pupil knows what to expect and what he or she has to do.

Access to the pair of comprehension questions is controlled by the pupil's success at reading the sentence. If the pupil makes one or two reading errors in a sentence, the questions may still be asked – but **not** if there are *more* than two errors.

To maintain the reading of a sentence, you may want to give the word over which a pupil stumbles. For the purposes of this test, **one word only** may be supplied and the comprehension questions still asked. If you have to supply more than one word, the comprehension questions cease to be a test of the pupil's own reading, so should not be asked.

If the pupil makes *one* error and is given *one* word (or vice versa), the comprehension questions may still be asked. If the pupil makes *two* errors and is given one word, do not ask the questions, as he/she is clearly struggling and is unlikely to get the questions right anyway.

Reading comprehension remains determined by reading accuracy: if a pupil cannot decode a sentence, he or she will be unable to do more than guess at its meaning. After the sixth error the testing may be stopped at any convenient place.

There are two boxes alongside each sentence in the Record Sheet in which to record whether the pupil answered each comprehension question correctly: these can be totalled at the foot of the page. We advise not waiting too long for a pupil to begin an answer (no more than 6 seconds) nor engaging in discussion before saying 'OK' and moving on.

Assessing progress

On **re-testing** with a different form of the test, you may wish to remind the pupil that they had read some sentences for you before, and that you are now going to ask them to read some new sentences to see how well they have been doing. There is space on the front of the Record Sheet to record the three assessments, A, B and C, so you can easily monitor progress over time.

We recommend that the separate forms be administered in the order A, B, C, and that *at least* six, or preferably twelve, months should elapse before the *same* form is re-used.

SCORING AND INTERPRETATION

The scoring system for the *New Salford* test is based on word-on-word progression through the 17 sentences. Each 'counted' word is shown in the Record Sheet in bold type and constitutes a discrete test item to be added to the reader's raw score total up to the point at which the sixth error is made.

1. The **reading age** norms for the test are contained on the Record Sheet: the figure displayed under the word on which a pupil makes their **sixth error** represents their reading age. This should be entered in the space provided on the front of the Record Sheet.

Where a pupil reads *all* of the sentences without making more than six errors, then the number of errors is used to derive a reading age. Thus, when all 17 sentences are completed with fewer than six errors, reading ages are given in Table 1.

Table 1: Reading ages for pupils who read all 114 words

Number of errors	Reading Age
5	10:11
4	10:11
3	11:0
2	11:1
1	11:2
0	11:3+

2. To obtain a **standardised score for reading accuracy**, first determine the total number of 'counted' words read to the place where the pupil made his or her sixth error. The running total of counted words is there to assist you. Then look up the age standardised score in Table A at the end of this manual. Standardised scores for pupils making fewer than six errors are given below word 114 at the foot of the table.

Note: for less able pupils aged 11:4 to 13:0, refer to Table B: this provides standardised scores in the below-average range.

3. To obtain **percentiles**, refer to the information on page 14.

4. The **comprehension age** is obtained by totalling the number of correct comprehension questions (literal and inferential) and referring to Table 2. If the pupil has not started with the easiest sentences – as many older pupils might – assume that all of the earlier comprehension questions were answered correctly.

Table 2: Comprehension age

Score	Comp. Age	Score	Comp. Age	Score	Comp. Age
		13	6:5	24	9:8
3 or fewer	<5:0	14	6:8	25	9:11
4	5:0	15	7:0	26	10:4
5	5:1	16	7:3	27	10:7
6	5:2	17	7:7	28	10:10
7	5:3	18	7:11	29	11:2
8	5:4	19	8:2	30	11:6
9	5:5	20	8:6	31	11:10
10	5:6	21	8:9	32	12:0
11	5:10	22	9:1	33	12:4
12	6:3	23	9:4	34	+12:7+

5. **Standardised scores for comprehension** may be obtained by reference to Table C, and for less able pupils aged 12:8 to 14 from Table D.

6. Some schools and teachers like to report performance against **National Curriculum sub-levels** to support the monitoring of reading progress. Tables 3a and 3b provide this information based on reading accuracy and comprehension, respectively. Note that these are *different* measures of reading ability, so the levels may not be the same.

Table 3a: Reading accuracy scores and National Curriculum levels

Reading Accuracy score (for 6th error)	Reading level
114 and 0 errors	6c+
114 and 1-2 errors	5a/b
114 and 3 errors	5c
114 and 4-6 errors	4a
113	4b
112	4c
110–111	3a
102–109	3b
96–101	3c
86–95	2a
74–85	2b
62–73	2c
49–61	1a
36–48	1b
26–35	1c
21–25	Wa
19–20	Wb
14–18	Wc
fewer than 13	below W

Table 3b: Comprehension scores and National Curriculum levels

Comprehension score	Reading level
34	6c+
33	5a
32	5b/c
31	4a
30	4b
28–29	4c
27	3a
26	3b
24–25	3c
22–23	2a
20–21	2b
17–19	2c
14–16	1a
10–13	1b
7–9	1c
6	Wa
4–5	Wb
3	Wc
1 or 2	below W

The graph in Figure 1 allows you to compare *reading accuracy* (i.e. the number of words read accurately) and *comprehension* (i.e. the number of comprehension questions answered correctly). A *photocopiable* version of this graph is provided on page 37.

Figure 1: Reading for meaning

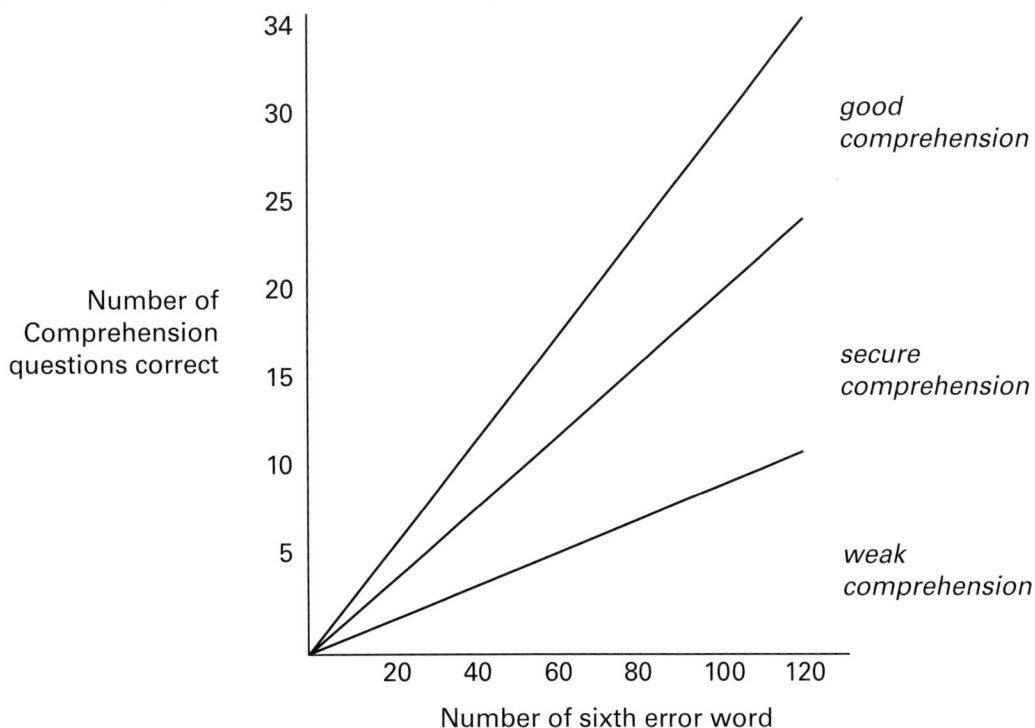

Number of Comprehension questions correct

Number of sixth error word

good comprehension

secure comprehension

weak comprehension

Plotting each child's scores on this graph highlights where those pupils who may be decoding and blending well may nevertheless be failing to *understand* what they are reading. If you are using all three forms of the test, you can plot each result in a different colour to enable you to see at a glance if the pupil is progressing from basic decoding and blending skills to true reading for meaning. Some pupils who are only able to read a few sentences may nevertheless understand what they have decoded and answer the comprehension questions correctly, such that – relative to their reading – their comprehension will show as excellent.

Percentiles can help to give you a better feel for the significance of a pupil's reading age, because they show the percentage in each age group who score below a certain level. So a standardised score at the 68th percentile means that 68 per cent of the group scored *below* that pupil's standardised score. Thus, that pupil is in the top third for his or her age group.

Percentile scores may be derived from standardised scores, for both reading accuracy and comprehension. To obtain a pupil's percentile, first calculate the pupil's chronological age and obtain his or her standardised score, as described above, and then refer to Table 4.

Table 4: Relationship between standardised scores and percentiles

Standardised Score	Percentile	Standardised Score	Percentile	Standardised Score	Percentile
130+	98+	108	70	89	24
128–9	97	107	68	88	22
126–7	96	106	66	87	20
125	95	105	63	86	18
123–4	94	104	60	85	16
122	93	103	58	84	14
121	92	102	55	83	13
120	91	101	52	82	12
119	90	100	50	81	11
118	89	99	48	80	9
117	87	98	45	79	8
116	86	97	42	78	7
115	84	96	40	76–7	6
114	82	95	37	75	5
113	80	94	34	73–4	4
112	78	93	32	71–2	3
111	77	92	30	70	2
110	74	91	28	70-	1
109	72	90	26		

The relationship between standardised scores and percentiles is most easily seen by reference to the normal distribution graph (Figure 2).

Figure 2: The normal distribution: standardised test scores and percentiles

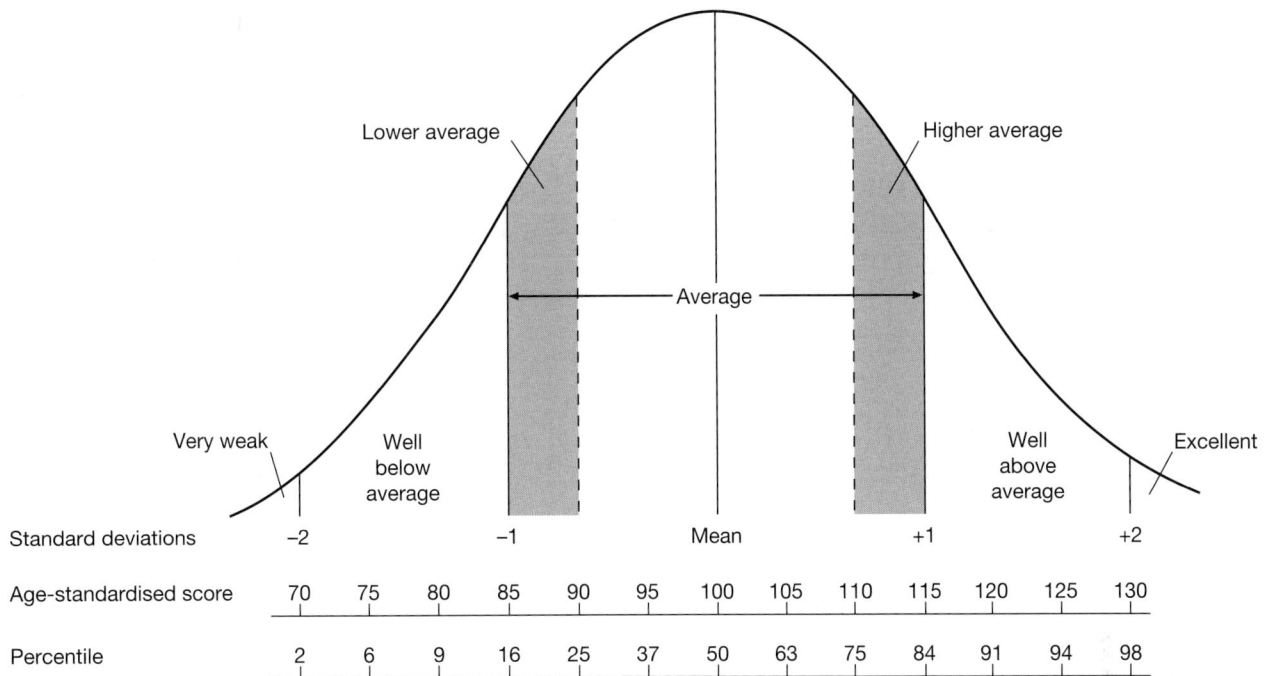

Standard deviations		−2		−1		Mean		+1		+2	
Age-standardised score	70	75	80	85	90	95	100	105	110	115	120	125	130
Percentile	2	6	9	16	25	37	50	63	75	84	91	94	98

Standardised score	Qualitative interpretation of standardised scores	Standard deviation from mean	Percentile score	Percentage of normal population
>130	Excellent	>+2	>98	2.27
116–130	Well above average	+1 to +2	84–98	13.59
110–115 85–115 85–90	higher average Average/age-appropriate lower average	−1 to +1	16–83	68.26
70–84	Well below average	−1 to −2	2–15	13.59
<69	Very weak	<−2	<2	2.27

Space is also provided on the Record Sheet to note how well a pupil engages with challenging text to make meaning and convey that meaning when reading aloud. Table 5 provides evidence from the standardisation trials against which to evaluate the pupil's performance when engaging with the three hardest sentences as they approach their 'decoding' ceiling.

Table 5: Subjective evaluation of pupils' reading, shown as a percentage

Reading Age	Reads fluently, with expression	Reads words well, but no flow to reading	Reads words, hesitating at times	Slowly forms words, blends phonemes	Can decode phonemes, but not blend
5:0–5:11	3%	7%	31%	50%	9%
6:0–6:11	6%	11%	46%	33%	4%
7:0–7:11	9%	17%	46%	24%	4%
8:0–8:11	17%	19%	49%	13%	2%
9:0–9:11	22%	20%	47%	10%	1%
10:0–10:11	36%	28%	30%	5%	1%

Above 11 years, pupils were almost all reading well or fluently.

DEVELOPMENT AND STANDARDISATION

In each of the three original (1976) Forms A, B and C, sentences in corresponding positions in the sequence of 13 were presented as having identical difficulty (i.e. the same reading ages were earned by pupils who made their sixth and final error on the nth sentence in either Form A, B or C). The original manual for the test implies this match was achieved through trial and error.

The interim revision carried out by Dennis Vincent and Mary Crumpler in 1998 omitted some of the original sentences which had become dated or used archaic vocabulary, but retained the remaining sentences virtually unchanged to create two forms X and Y. Updated norms for these two forms were established via a process of calibration against nationally standardised *group* tests, as described in the second (1998) and third (2002) editions of the manual.

In the early trialling process for the *New Salford Sentence Reading Test* we created three forms as described on page 6, and monitored children's performance on two forms, A and B or A and C taken immediately after each other (except with Years 1 and 2) to see where pupils reached the sixth error. This gave us confidence to anticipate that in the standardisation all three forms would perform similarly.

The 2011 standardisation

Over 9200 pupils in a total of 70 schools (including ten secondary schools and two special schools, together with a number of schools visited by members of a local authority Learning Support Service) were involved in the trials, which took place during late September and October 2011. Schools from England, Wales, Northern and Southern Ireland participated. Pupil numbers for each year are shown in Table 6, and Table 7 shows demographic information about the participating schools.

Many of the schools were familiar with using the previous version of 'Salford' to monitor progress of poor readers. These schools in the current standardisation sample normally used the 'New Salford' with all of the pupils in the primary schools or, usually, across the whole of a year group in the secondary schools. In total 18203 tests were taken and used in the standardisation. We are thus confident that the norms and statistics obtained are secure in terms of the sample being a reasonable subset of the whole school population.

Table 6: Numbers of pupils in each year group

	Y1	Y2	Y3	Y4	Y5	Y6	Y7	Y8	Y9	Y10
Girls	618	625	713	630	517	547	400	206	146	39
Boys	596	679	772	653	584	547	488	226	150	43
Totals*	1223	1307	1498	1283	1108	1095	890	436	296	84

*Twelve reception children also took part, and across the years 41 had no gender provided for classification. Most pupils took either Form A and Form B, or Form A and Form C.

Table 7: Demographic school information

Central in large town/city	Suburban to town/city	Rural small town	Village
13	19	19	19
Only English as first language	Fewer than 5 different home languages	Between 6–19 different home languages	More than 20 home languages
14	28	20	8

Reading and comprehension ages, and NC levels

Reading ages for a test can be derived in a number of ways, and different methods tend to give slightly different equivalences between test scores and age values. The reading age we use is that of the 50th percentile – i.e. the average age of the pupils who got that score as their average mark.

The comprehension age was also obtained from the 50th percentile, except for chronological ages below 6, when average age for each score is reported.

National Curriculum levels are most secure at the end of the Summer term. For this reason, the equivalences given in Tables 3a and 3b refer to the level the pupil had been awarded at the end of the Summer term prior to the standardisation trials at the beginning of October.

Reliability and validity

The original 1976 *Salford* manual reported correlations of 0.95+ between the three forms of the test, and 'predictive reliability' (test-retest) of over 0.95. Correlations with a range of contemporarily published tests of reading and spelling in excess of 0.9 are also reported, together with slightly lower values for groups in low/restricted ability ranges. The size of samples involved in any one of the correlations reported tends to be quite small, but nevertheless the overall evidence provides reasonably robust support for the concurrent validity of the original tests.

There is every reason to believe that the original evidence would apply to the tests in their current form as the statistical measures – Pearson's age correlation and Cronbach's α – both indicate a very high reliability for the *New Salford Sentence Reading Test* for all three forms (see Table 8).

Table 8: Reliability measures

	Pearson correlation of age with word score	Cronbach alpha	90% confidence band
Form A	0.70	0.99	+/-4.94
Form B	0.70	0.99	+/-4.99
Form C	0.72	0.99	+/-4.94

In the standardisation trials, all pupils took Form A. One half also took Form B, and the other half took Form C. All pupils did Form A first and then met either Form B or C within a fortnight. It was deemed unnecessary to try to balance the order of the testing, as the three forms have different sentences, so there is unlikely to be any learning from the first experience to influence the second.

Analysis by equipercentile equating showed that Forms B and C may be up to two words harder than Form A across the lower and middle range of scores. The slight differences are accommodated on the Record Sheet for Forms B and C, where the reading ages have been linearly equated word-for-word to Form A. This has no effect on the standardised scores, which are based on the total standardisation test data.

The 90% confidence band for the tests is plus or minus 5 points of standardised score – so for a pupil with a standardised score of, say, 105 you can be 90% confident that their 'true' standardised score is between 100 and 110. The internal reliability shown by Cronbach alpha is exceptionally high.

Standardisation and norms

The *New Salford Sentence Reading Test* norms are based on much larger numbers than its previous versions. It is not possible to make direct comparisons between this *New Salford* and previous versions, as the number of sentences has increased from 13 to 17 and the content of many of the sentences has altered too. However, a number of the words and phrases in the previous revision are also present in this new version.

Table 9 illustrates the reading ages associated with pupils making their sixth error on these words and phrases. As may be seen by inspection, there is an extremely close match indicating that the standard of the *New Salford* is similar to the previous *Salford*, while extending the reading ages beyond 10:6 with the harder final two sentences.

The *New Salford* may also be more reliable at the lower reading ages, as the two extra sentences here enable more accurate reading ages to be determined, and this, together with the modification of many sentences to provide more accessible language, has increased the validity of the test.

Table 9

Word groups present in previous and New Salford	2002 reading age	2011 reading age
Form X with Form A		
The robber tried to hide but the police found him	4:9–5:4	5:3–5:6
received tremendous applause for performance	8:0–8:4	8:0–8:3
hesitated before… announcing decision	8:5–8:6; 8:8–8:9	8:5–8:6; 8:6–8:7
exhibition	9:7	9:7
Form Y with Form A		
He got some sweets from the shop	4:3	<4:5
ready quickly… catch… eight o'clock	5:5–5:6; 5:10; 6:0–6:1	5:9–5:10; 5:10; 5:11–6:0
Form X with Form B		
Come and play ball	4:3	<4:5
We like to make things at school	4:3	<4:5
Form Y with Form B		
trouble	6:11	6:11
injured ankle while attempting… escape	7:0–7:5	6:11–7:3
Although exhausted… refused to accompany… rescuers	8:0–8:5	8:1–8:4
Assistance… requested… survivors… earthquake	8:5–9:3	8:6–8:9
entertainment	9:9	9:11
Form X with Form C		
busy traffic speeding	5:7–5:9	5:11–6:0
described… happened	7:0; 7:3	7:2; 7:5
huge population	7:9–7:10	7:8–7:9
Form Y with Form C		
flowers… garden	4:6; 4:9	4:9; 4:10
Robert kicked the door and broke the glass	4:9–5:4	5:5–5:8
restaurant… reputation	10:0; 10:3	9:6; 9:7

A number of schools provided a comparison of *reading ages* obtained in the 2011 trials with those obtained using the 2002 version of the test. Direct comparison is difficult because of the changes to the test content (see page 6), but allowing for the number of months elapsed between the two tests, and omitting the ceiling effects, the reading ages from the trials were on average 2–3 months higher. We are confident that the *New Salford* is not easier per se, but there are now more sentences that are appropriate to pupils of differing ability. Also the contexts, syntax and vocabulary are better matched to where pupils are in their progress in reading. This increased accessibility has enabled the pupils to read further through the sentences before making their sixth error. Because of this better match to each pupil's learning experience, we believe the *New Salford* to be a more valid test.

As may be seen from Table 10, almost all pupils – over 90% – read the first 13 words correctly and most read the first 17 counting words correctly. Because of this high degree of success with the easier words and the strong correlation of age to performance, we were able to extrapolate the reading ages down below age 5 to aid differentiation among the weakest readers.

Table 10: Facilities for words in Form A (percentage of pupils reading each word correctly)

Word	Facility	Word	Facility	Word	Facility
my	96%	quickly	74%	trick	53%
pen	99%	catch	75%	hesitated	39%
is	99%	eight	71%	before	50%
red	99%	o'clock	74%	announcing	46%
pick	94%	still	74%	decision	40%
up	99%	arrive	71%	class	47%
a	99%	work	73%	prize	46%
book	93%	time	74%	good	46%
we	95%	field	67%	behaviour	46%
must	93%	peas	67%	global	39%
home	93%	been	72%	communication	34%
dinner	90%	picked	70%	incredibly	37%
now	89%	important	69%	successful	39%
some	92%	freeze	70%	result	40%
sweets	87%	very	70%	development	34%
from	91%	swiftly	63%	internet	38%
shop	93%	gripped	62%	museum	38%
extra	75%	branches	65%	hosting	35%
music	78%	climbed	67%	exhibition	24%
lesson	81%	began	66%	historic	33%
football	83%	worrying	66%	contemporary	22%
after	83%	about	68%	paintings	33%
break	79%	how	68%	January	33%
travels	75%	down	68%	fund-raising	33%
school	82%	realising	38%	events	33%
taxi	80%	finally	64%	government	32%
with	82%	won	66%	grants	32%
two	81%	writing	64%	enabled	27%
younger	75%	competition	63%	purchase	26%
sisters	79%	James	65%	expand	29%
robber	74%	grinned	59%	grounds	30%
tried	75%	ear	63%	prestigious	9%
hide	76%	magician	40%	orchestra	18%
police	76%	receive	43%	require	24%
found	77%	tremendous	38%	expert	24%
stolen	74%	applause	42%	musicians	22%
money	76%	perform	51%	conductor	22%
ready	72%	new	53%	rehearse	21%

TABLE A: Standardised scores for reading accuracy

Age in years and completed months

(Blank cells in the upper-right region are marked "SCORE 70- IN THIS AREA".)

6th error word	5:6	5:7	5:8	5:9	5:10	5:11	6:0	6:1	6:2	6:3	6:4	6:5	6:6	6:7	6:8	6:9	6:10	6:11	7:0	7:1	7:2	7:3	7:4	7:5	6th error word
6	81	81	78	77	75	70																			6
7	82	81	79	78	76	72																			7
8	83	82	80	79	77	74	70																		8
9	83	82	81	80	78	77	72	70																	9
10	85	83	82	81	79	78	74	71																	10
11	85	85	83	82	81	80	75	74																	11
12	86	85	84	83	82	81	78	76	70																12
13	87	86	85	84	83	82	81	78	73	70															13
14	87	87	86	85	84	83	82	81	76	72	70														14
15	88	87	86	86	85	84	83	82	78	77	71	70													15
16	89	88	87	86	85	85	84	83	80	79	75	71	70												16
17	89	88	88	87	86	85	84	83	82	80	77	76	73	70											17
18	90	89	88	87	87	86	85	84	82	81	79	77	76	71	70										18
19	90	90	89	88	87	87	86	85	83	82	80	79	77	74	72	70									19
20	91	90	89	89	88	87	86	86	84	83	81	80	79	76	75	71	70								20
21	92	91	90	89	89	88	87	86	85	84	82	81	80	77	76	73	72	70							21
22	92	92	91	90	89	88	88	87	86	85	83	82	81	78	77	75	74	71	70						22
23	93	92	91	91	90	89	88	87	86	85	84	83	82	79	78	76	76	73	71	70					23
24	94	93	92	91	90	90	89	88	87	86	85	84	83	80	79	78	77	74	73	71					24
25	94	93	93	92	91	90	89	89	87	87	85	85	84	81	80	79	78	75	75	72	70				25
26	95	94	93	92	92	91	90	89	88	87	86	86	85	82	81	80	79	76	76	74	71				26
27	95	95	94	93	92	91	91	90	89	88	87	86	85	83	82	81	80	77	77	75	73	70			27
28	96	95	94	94	93	92	91	90	89	88	88	87	86	85	83	82	81	78	78	76	74	71			28
29	97	96	95	94	93	92	92	91	90	89	88	87	87	85	84	83	82	79	79	77	75	73	70		29
30	97	97	96	95	94	93	92	92	91	90	89	88	87	86	85	84	83	80	80	78	76	74	71	70	30
31	98	97	96	96	95	93	93	92	91	91	90	89	88	87	85	85	84	82	81	79	77	75	72	71	31
32	99	98	97	96	95	94	94	93	92	91	90	90	88	88	86	85	85	83	82	80	78	76	73	72	32
33	99	98	98	97	96	95	94	94	93	92	91	90	89	88	87	86	85	84	82	81	79	77	74	73	33
34	100	99	98	97	97	95	95	94	93	93	92	91	90	89	87	87	86	84	83	81	80	78	75	74	34
35	100	100	99	98	97	96	96	95	94	93	92	92	90	89	88	87	86	85	84	82	81	79	76	75	35
36	101	100	99	99	98	96	96	95	95	94	93	92	91	90	89	88	87	86	84	83	81	80	77	76	36
37	102	101	100	99	98	97	97	96	95	94	94	93	91	91	89	89	88	87	85	84	82	81	78	77	37
38	102	101	101	100	99	98	98	97	96	95	94	93	92	91	90	89	88	87	85	85	83	82	79	78	38
39	103	101	101	101	100	98	98	97	97	96	95	94	93	92	90	90	89	88	86	85	84	83	80	79	39
40	103	102	102	101	100	99	99	98	97	96	96	95	93	92	91	91	89	89	87	86	85	83	81	80	40
41	104	103	102	102	101	99	99	99	98	97	96	95	94	93	92	91	90	90	88	87	86	84	82	81	41
42	105	103	103	103	102	100	100	99	99	98	97	96	95	94	93	92	91	90	89	88	87	85	83	82	42
43	105	104	104	103	102	100	101	100	99	98	98	97	95	94	93	93	91	91	89	88	88	86	84	83	43
44	106	104	104	104	103	101	101	101	100	99	98	97	96	95	94	93	92	92	90	89	89	87	85	84	44
45	107	105	105	105	103	101	102	101	100	100	99	98	96	96	95	94	93	92	91	90	90	88	86	85	45
46	107	106	106	105	104	102	103	102	101	100	99	98	97	96	95	95	93	93	92	91	91	89	87	86	46
47	108	107	106	106	105	103	103	102	102	101	100	99	98	97	96	95	94	94	92	92	92	90	88	87	47
48	108	107	107	107	105	104	104	103	102	102	101	100	99	98	97	96	95	95	93	93	93	91	89	88	48
49	109	108	108	107	106	105	104	104	103	102	101	100	99	99	98	97	96	95	94	93	93	92	90	89	49
50	110	109	108	108	107	106	105	104	103	103	102	101	100	100	99	98	97	96	95	94	94	93	92	91	50
6th error word	5:6	5:7	5:8	5:9	5:10	5:11	6:0	6:1	6:2	6:3	6:4	6:5	6:6	6:7	6:8	6:9	6:10	6:11	7:0	7:1	7:2	7:3	7:4	7:5	6th error word

	7:5	7:4	7:3	7:2	7:1	7:0	6:11	6:10	6:9	6:8	6:7	6:6	6:5	6:4	6:3	6:2	6:1	6:0	5:11	5:10	5:9	5:8	5:7	5:6	
51	92	93	93	94	95	96	97	98	99	99	100	101	102	103	103	104	105	106	107	107	108	109	110	111	51
52	92	93	94	95	96	97	98	98	99	100	101	102	103	103	104	105	106	107	107	108	109	110	111	111	52
53	93	94	95	96	96	97	98	99	100	101	102	102	103	104	105	106	107	107	108	109	110	111	111	112	53
54	94	95	95	96	97	98	99	100	101	101	102	103	104	105	106	106	107	108	109	110	110	111	112	113	54
55	94	95	96	97	98	99	100	100	101	102	103	104	105	106	106	107	108	109	110	110	111	112	113	113	55
56	95	96	97	98	99	99	100	101	102	103	104	104	105	106	107	108	109	110	110	111	112	113	113	113	56
57	96	97	98	98	99	100	101	102	103	103	104	105	106	107	108	108	109	110	111	112	113	113	113	114	57
58	96	97	98	99	100	101	102	103	104	104	105	106	107	108	108	109	110	111	112	113	113	113	114	114	58
59	97	98	99	100	101	102	102	103	105	105	106	107	107	108	109	109	111	111	113	113	114	114	114	115	59
60	98	99	100	100	101	102	103	104	105	106	107	107	108	109	110	110	112	112	113	114	114	114	115	115	60
61	99	99	100	101	102	103	104	105	106	107	107	108	109	110	111	111	112	113	114	114	115	115	115	116	61
62	99	100	101	102	103	104	105	106	106	107	108	109	110	111	112	112	113	113	114	115	115	116	116	116	62
63	100	101	102	103	103	104	105	106	107	108	109	110	111	112	112	112	113	114	115	115	116	116	117	117	63
64	101	102	102	103	104	105	106	107	108	109	110	110	112	112	113	113	114	114	115	116	116	117	117	117	64
65	101	102	103	104	105	106	107	108	109	110	111	111	112	113	113	113	114	115	116	116	117	118	118	118	65
66	102	103	104	105	106	107	108	109	110	111	111	112	113	113	114	114	115	115	116	117	118	118	118	119	66
67	103	104	105	106	107	108	108	110	111	111	112	113	113	114	114	114	115	116	117	118	118	119	119	119	67
68	104	105	106	107	107	108	109	110	111	112	113	113	114	114	115	115	116	116	118	118	119	118	119	120	68
69	104	106	107	107	108	109	109	111	112	113	113	114	114	115	115	116	116	117	118	119	120	119	120	121	69
70	105	106	107	108	109	110	110	112	113	113	114	114	115	115	116	117	117	118	119	119	120	120	121	121	70
71	106	107	108	109	110	111	111	113	113	114	114	115	115	116	117	117	118	119	120	120	121	121	121	122	71
72	107	108	109	110	111	112	112	113	114	114	115	115	116	117	117	118	119	119	120	120	122	121	122	122	72
73	108	109	110	111	112	113	113	114	115	115	115	116	117	117	118	119	119	120	121	121	123	122	123	123	73
74	109	110	111	112	113	113	114	114	115	115	116	117	117	118	119	119	120	121	122	122	123	123	123	124	74
75	110	111	112	113	113	114	114	115	116	116	117	117	118	119	119	120	121	121	122	123	124	123	124	124	75
76	111	112	113	113	114	114	115	115	117	117	118	118	119	120	120	121	122	122	123	124	125	124	124	125	76
77	112	113	113	114	115	115	115	116	118	118	118	119	120	120	121	121	123	123	124	124	126	125	125	126	77
78	113	113	114	114	115	115	116	117	119	118	119	120	120	121	122	122	123	123	124	125	126	125	126	127	78
79	113	114	114	115	116	116	117	118	119	119	120	121	121	122	122	123	124	124	125	126	127	126	127	127	79
80	114	114	115	115	116	117	118	119	120	120	121	121	122	122	123	124	125	125	126	127	128	127	127	128	80
81	114	115	116	116	117	118	119	119	121	121	121	122	123	123	124	124	126	125	127	128	129	128	128	129	81
82	115	116	116	117	118	119	120	120	122	122	122	123	123	124	124	125	127	126	128	128	130	129	128	130	82
83	116	116	117	118	119	120	120	121	122	122	123	124	124	125	125	126	127	127	129	129		129	129		83
84	117	117	118	119	120	120	121	122	123	123	124	124	125	126	126	127	128	128	130	130		130	130		84
85	117	118	119	120	121	121	122	123	124	124	124	125	126	126	127	128	129	129							85
86	118	119	120	121	121	122	123	123	125	125	125	126	127	127	128	129	130	130							86
87	119	120	121	122	122	123	124	124	126	126	126	127	128	128	129	130									87
88	120	121	122	122	123	124	124	125	127	127	127	128	129	129	130	130									88
89	121	122	122	123	124	125	125	126	128	128	128	129	129	130											89
90	122	123	123	124	125	126	126	127	129	129	129	130	130												90
91	123	124	124	125	126	127	128	128	130	130	130														91
92	124	125	124	126	127	128	129	129																	92
93	125	126	125	127	128	129	130	130																	93
94	126	127	127	129	129	130											SCORE 130+ IN THIS AREA								94
95	127	128	128	130	130																				95
96	129	129	129																						96
97	130		130																						97
	7:5	7:4	7:3	7:2	7:1	7:0	6:11	6:10	6:9	6:8	6:7	6:6	6:5	6:4	6:3	6:2	6:1	6:0	5:11	5:10	5:9	5:8	5:7	5:6	

TABLE A cont

6th error word	Age in years and completed months																							6th error word
	7:6	7:7	7:8	7:9	7:10	7:11	8:0	8:1	8:2	8:3	8:4	8:5	8:6	8:7	8:8	8:9	8:10	8:11	9:0	9:1	9:2	9:3	9:4	9:5	
20	70	70																							20
21	71	71	70													SCORE 70- IN THIS AREA									21
22	72	72	71	71	70	70																			22
23	73	73	72	71	71	71	70	70																	23
24	74	73	73	72	72	71	71	71	70	70															24
25	75	74	74	73	73	72	72	71	71	71	70	70													25
26	76	75	75	74	73	73	72	72	72	71	71	71	70	70											26
27	77	76	75	75	74	74	73	73	72	72	72	71	71	71	70	70									27
28	78	77	76	76	75	74	74	73	73	73	72	72	71	71	71	71	70	70							28
29	78	78	77	76	76	75	75	74	74	73	73	72	72	72	71	71	71	71	70	70					29
30	79	78	78	77	76	76	75	75	74	74	73	73	73	72	72	72	71	71	71	71	70	70	70		30
31	80	79	78	78	77	76	76	75	75	74	74	74	73	73	72	72	72	72	71	71	71	71	70	70	31
32	81	80	79	78	78	77	77	76	76	75	75	74	74	73	73	73	72	72	72	72	71	71	71	71	32
33	81	81	80	79	78	78	77	77	76	76	75	75	74	74	74	73	73	73	72	72	72	71	71	71	33
34	82	81	81	80	79	78	78	77	77	76	76	75	75	74	74	74	73	73	73	72	72	72	72	71	34
35	82	82	81	81	80	79	79	78	77	77	76	76	75	75	75	74	74	73	73	73	73	72	72	72	35
36	83	82	82	81	81	80	79	79	78	77	77	76	76	76	75	75	74	74	74	73	73	73	72	72	36
37	84	83	82	82	81	81	80	79	79	78	77	77	76	76	76	75	75	74	74	74	73	73	73	73	37
38	84	83	83	82	82	81	80	80	79	79	78	78	77	77	76	76	75	75	75	74	74	74	73	73	38
39	85	84	83	83	82	82	81	80	80	79	79	78	78	77	77	76	76	75	75	75	74	74	74	73	39
40	85	85	84	83	83	82	82	81	80	80	79	79	78	78	77	77	76	76	75	75	75	74	74	74	40
41	86	85	84	84	83	83	82	81	81	80	80	79	79	78	78	77	77	76	76	76	75	75	75	74	41
42	86	85	85	84	84	83	83	82	81	81	80	80	79	79	78	78	77	77	76	76	76	75	75	75	42
43	87	86	85	85	84	84	83	82	82	81	81	80	80	79	79	78	78	77	77	77	76	76	75	75	43
44	87	86	86	85	85	84	84	83	82	82	81	81	80	80	79	79	78	78	77	77	77	76	76	75	44
45	88	87	86	86	85	85	84	83	83	82	82	81	81	80	80	79	79	78	78	77	77	77	76	76	45
46	88	87	87	86	86	85	85	84	83	83	82	82	81	81	80	80	79	79	78	78	77	77	77	76	46
47	89	88	87	87	86	86	85	84	84	83	83	82	82	81	81	80	80	79	79	78	78	78	77	77	47
48	89	89	88	87	87	86	85	85	84	84	83	83	82	82	81	81	80	80	79	79	78	78	78	77	48
49	90	89	88	88	87	86	86	85	85	84	84	83	83	82	82	81	81	80	80	79	79	78	78	78	49
50	90	90	89	88	88	87	86	86	85	85	84	84	83	83	82	82	81	81	80	80	79	79	78	78	50
51	91	90	89	89	88	87	87	86	86	85	85	84	84	83	83	82	82	81	81	80	80	79	79	78	51
52	92	91	90	89	89	88	87	87	86	86	85	85	84	83	83	82	82	82	81	81	80	80	79	79	52
53	92	91	91	90	89	88	88	87	87	86	85	85	84	84	83	83	82	82	82	81	81	80	80	79	53
54	93	92	91	90	90	89	88	88	87	86	86	85	85	84	84	83	83	82	82	81	81	81	80	80	54
55	93	93	92	91	90	89	89	88	87	87	86	86	85	85	84	84	83	83	82	82	81	81	81	80	55
56	94	93	92	92	91	90	89	89	88	87	87	86	86	85	85	84	84	83	83	82	82	81	81	81	56
57	95	94	93	92	91	91	90	89	88	88	87	87	86	86	85	85	84	84	83	83	82	82	81	81	57
58	95	95	94	93	92	91	90	90	89	88	88	87	87	86	85	85	84	84	84	83	83	82	82	81	58
59	96	95	94	94	93	92	91	90	90	89	88	88	87	86	86	85	85	84	84	83	83	83	82	82	59
60	97	96	95	94	93	92	92	91	90	89	89	88	87	87	86	86	85	85	84	84	83	83	83	82	60
61	98	97	96	95	94	93	92	91	91	90	89	89	88	87	87	86	86	85	85	84	84	83	83	82	61
62	98	97	96	96	95	94	93	92	91	91	90	89	88	88	87	87	86	86	85	85	84	84	83	83	62
63	99	98	97	96	95	94	94	93	92	91	90	90	89	88	88	87	87	86	86	85	85	84	84	83	63
64	100	99	98	97	96	95	94	93	93	92	91	90	89	89	88	87	87	86	86	85	85	84	84	84	64
65	100	100	99	98	97	96	95	94	93	92	92	91	90	89	89	88	87	87	86	86	85	85	84	84	65
	7:6	7:7	7:8	7:9	7:10	7:11	8:0	8:1	8:2	8:3	8:4	8:5	8:6	8:7	8:8	8:9	8:10	8:11	9:0	9:1	9:2	9:3	9:4	9:5	

	9:5	9:4	9:3	9:2	9:1	9:0	8:11	8:10	8:9	8:8	8:7	8:6	8:5	8:4	8:3	8:2	8:1	8:0	7:11	7:10	7:9	7:8	7:7	7:6	
66	84	85	85	86	86	87	87	88	88	89	90	91	91	92	93	94	95	96	97	98	99	99	100	101	66
67	85	85	86	86	87	87	88	88	89	90	90	91	92	93	94	95	95	96	97	98	99	100	101	102	67
68	85	86	86	87	87	88	88	89	89	90	91	92	93	93	94	95	96	97	98	99	100	101	102	103	68
69	85	86	86	87	87	88	89	89	90	91	92	92	93	94	95	96	97	98	99	100	101	102	103	103	69
70	86	86	87	88	88	89	89	90	91	91	92	93	94	95	96	97	98	99	100	101	102	102	103	104	70
71	86	87	88	88	88	90	90	90	92	92	93	94	95	96	97	98	98	99	100	101	102	103	104	105	71
72	87	87	88	89	89	90	90	91	92	93	94	94	95	96	97	98	99	100	101	102	103	104	105	106	72
73	87	88	88	89	89	91	91	92	93	93	94	95	96	97	98	99	100	101	102	103	104	105	106	107	73
74	87	88	89	89	90	91	91	92	94	94	95	96	97	98	99	100	101	102	103	104	105	106	107	108	74
75	88	88	89	90	90	92	92	93	95	95	96	97	98	99	100	101	102	103	103	105	106	107	108	109	75
76	88	89	90	90	91	93	93	94	95	95	96	97	98	99	100	101	102	103	104	106	107	108	109	110	76
77	89	89	90	91	92	93	93	94	96	96	97	98	99	100	101	102	103	104	105	106	107	108	110	111	77
78	89	90	91	92	92	94	94	95	97	97	98	99	100	101	102	103	104	105	106	107	108	110	111	112	78
79	90	91	91	92	93	95	95	96	98	98	99	100	101	102	103	104	105	106	107	108	109	111	112	113	79
80	90	91	92	93	94	95	96	97	98	99	100	101	102	103	104	105	106	107	108	109	111	112	113	113	80
81	91	92	93	93	94	96	96	97	99	99	100	102	103	103	105	106	107	108	109	110	111	113	113	114	81
82	92	92	93	94	95	97	97	98	100	100	101	103	103	104	106	107	108	109	110	111	112	114	114	114	82
83	92	93	94	95	96	98	98	99	101	101	102	103	104	105	107	108	109	110	111	112	113	115	114	115	83
84	93	94	95	96	97	98	99	100	102	102	103	104	105	106	108	109	110	111	112	113	114	116	115	116	84
85	94	94	95	96	98	99	100	101	103	103	104	105	106	107	109	110	111	112	113	114	114	117	116	117	85
86	94	95	96	97	98	99	100	102	103	104	105	106	107	107	110	111	112	113	114	114	115	118	117	118	86
87	95	96	97	98	99	100	101	102	105	105	106	107	108	109	111	112	113	114	114	115	116	119	118	118	87
88	96	97	98	99	100	101	102	103	106	106	107	108	110	110	112	113	114	114	115	116	117	120	119	119	88
89	97	98	99	100	101	102	103	104	107	107	108	110	111	111	113	114	115	115	116	117	118	121	120	120	89
90	97	99	100	101	102	103	104	106	108	108	109	111	112	112	114	115	116	116	117	118	119	122	121	121	90
91	98	99	100	102	103	104	105	107	109	109	111	112	113	113	114	116	117	117	118	119	120	123	122	122	91
92	99	100	101	103	104	105	107	108	111	111	112	113	114	114	115	117	118	118	119	120	121	124	122	123	92
93	100	101	102	104	105	106	108	109	112	112	113	114	114	115	116	118	119	119	120	121	122	125	123	124	93
94	101	102	103	105	106	107	109	110	113	113	114	114	115	116	117	119	120	120	121	122	123	126	124	125	94
95	102	103	105	106	107	109	110	112	114	114	115	116	116	116	118	121	122	121	122	123	124	127	126	126	95
96	103	104	106	107	109	110	112	113	115	115	115	118	117	117	120	122	123	122	123	124	126	129	127	128	96
97	104	106	107	108	110	112	113	114	115	117	116	119	119	119	121	123	124	124	124	125	128	130	128	129	97
98	105	107	108	110	111	113	114	115	117	118	118	120	120	120	122	124	125	125	126	127	129		129	129	98
99	107	108	110	111	113	114	115	115	118	119	119	121	121	121	123	125	126	126	127	128	130			130	99
100	108	110	111	113	114	115	117	117	119	121	120	123	122	122	124	127	128	128	129	129					100
101	109	111	113	114	115	115	118	118	121	122	122	124	124	123	126	128	129	129	130						101
102	111	113	114	115	115	117	120	120	122	123	123	126	125	125	127	130		130							102
103	113	114	115	116	117	118	121	121	124	125	124	127	127	126	129										103
104	114	115	116	117	119	120	122	122	125	127	126	129	128	128											104
105	115	116	117	119	120	122	123	124	127	128	128		130	130											105
106	116	117	119	120	122	123	124	126	129	130	130														106
107	118	119	121	122	123	125	126	128																	107
108	119	121	122	124	125	127	128	130																	108
109	121	123	124	126	128	129	130																		109
110	123	125	127	128	130																				110
111	125	127	129																						111
112	128	130																							112
113																									113
	9:5	9:4	9:3	9:2	9:1	9:0	8:11	8:10	8:9	8:8	8:7	8:6	8:5	8:4	8:3	8:2	8:1	8:0	7:11	7:10	7:9	7:8	7:7	7:6	

SCORE 130+ IN THIS AREA

TABLE A cont

Age in years and completed months

6th error word	9:6	9:7	9:8	9:9	9:10	9:11	10:0	10:1	10:2	10:3	10:4	10:5	10:6	10:7	10:8	10:9	10:10	10:11	11:0	11:1	11:2	11:3	6th error word
30	70																						30
31	70	70	70																				31
32	70	70	70	70	70																		32
33	71	71	70	70	70	70	70	70															33
34	71	71	71	70	70	70	70	70	70														34
35	72	71	71	71	71	70	70	70	70	70	70	70											35
36	72	72	72	71	71	71	71	71	70	70	70	70	70	70									36
37	72	72	72	71	71	71	71	71	71	70	70	70	70	70	70	70							37
38	73	72	72	72	72	71	71	71	71	71	71	71	70	70	70	70	70						38
39	73	73	72	72	72	72	72	72	71	71	71	71	70	71	70	70	70	70	70				39
40	74	73	73	72	73	72	72	72	72	72	71	71	71	71	71	71	70	70	70	70	70		40
41	74	73	73	73	73	72	72	72	72	72	72	72	71	71	71	71	71	70	70	70	70	70	41
42	74	74	74	73	73	73	73	73	72	72	72	72	72	72	71	71	71	71	71	70	70	70	42
43	75	74	74	73	74	73	73	73	73	73	72	72	72	72	72	72	71	71	71	71	71	70	43
44	75	74	74	74	74	74	74	73	73	73	73	72	72	72	72	72	72	71	71	71	71	70	44
45	76	75	75	74	74	74	74	74	73	73	73	73	72	73	72	72	72	71	72	71	71	71	45
46	76	75	75	75	75	74	74	74	74	73	73	73	73	73	72	72	72	72	72	71	71	71	46
47	77	76	75	75	75	75	75	74	74	74	74	73	73	73	73	73	72	72	72	72	72	71	47
48	77	76	76	75	75	75	75	75	74	74	74	74	73	74	73	73	73	72	72	72	72	72	48
49	77	76	76	76	76	76	75	75	75	74	74	74	74	74	73	73	73	73	73	72	72	72	49
50	78	77	77	76	76	76	76	75	75	75	75	74	74	74	74	73	73	73	73	72	72	72	50
51	78	77	77	77	77	76	76	76	75	75	75	75	74	75	74	74	73	73	73	73	73	72	51
52	78	78	78	77	77	77	76	76	76	75	75	75	75	75	74	74	74	73	73	73	73	73	52
53	79	78	78	77	77	77	77	76	76	76	76	75	75	75	75	74	74	74	74	73	73	73	53
54	79	78	78	78	78	78	77	77	76	76	76	76	75	75	75	75	74	74	74	74	74	73	54
55	80	79	79	78	78	78	78	77	77	77	76	76	76	76	75	75	75	74	74	74	74	73	55
56	80	79	79	79	79	78	78	77	77	77	77	76	76	76	75	75	75	74	75	74	74	74	56
57	81	80	79	79	79	79	78	78	78	77	77	77	76	76	76	75	75	75	75	74	74	74	57
58	81	80	80	79	79	79	79	78	78	78	77	77	77	77	76	76	76	75	75	75	75	74	58
59	81	80	80	80	80	79	79	79	78	78	78	77	77	77	76	76	76	76	75	75	75	75	59
60	82	81	81	80	80	80	79	79	79	78	78	78	77	77	77	76	76	76	76	75	75	75	60
61	82	81	81	80	80	80	80	79	79	79	78	78	78	78	77	77	77	76	76	76	75	75	61
62	82	82	82	81	81	80	80	80	79	79	79	78	78	78	77	77	77	77	76	76	76	76	62
63	83	82	82	81	81	81	80	80	80	79	79	79	78	78	78	77	77	77	77	76	76	76	63
64	83	82	82	82	82	81	81	80	80	80	79	79	79	79	78	78	77	77	77	77	76	76	64
65	84	83	83	82	82	82	81	81	80	80	80	79	79	79	78	78	78	77	77	77	77	76	65
66	84	83	83	82	82	82	81	81	81	80	80	80	79	79	79	78	78	78	78	77	77	77	66
67	84	83	83	83	83	82	82	81	81	81	80	80	80	80	79	78	78	78	78	78	77	77	67
68	85	84	84	83	83	83	82	82	81	81	81	80	80	80	79	79	79	78	78	78	78	77	68
69	85	84	84	83	83	83	82	82	82	81	81	81	80	80	79	79	79	79	79	78	78	78	69
70	85	85	84	84	84	83	83	82	82	82	81	81	81	81	80	79	79	79	79	78	78	78	70
71	86	85	85	84	84	84	83	83	82	82	81	81	81	81	80	80	80	79	79	79	79	78	71
72	86	86	85	85	84	84	84	83	83	82	82	82	81	82	81	80	80	80	80	79	79	78	72
73	87	86	86	85	85	84	84	83	83	83	82	82	82	82	81	80	80	80	80	80	79	79	73
74	87	86	86	85	85	85	84	84	84	83	83	82	82	82	81	81	81	80	80	80	79	79	74
75	87	87	86	86	85	85	85	84	84	83	83	83	82	82	82	81	81	81	80	80	80	79	75
6th error word	9:6	9:7	9:8	9:9	9:10	9:11	10:0	10:1	10:2	10:3	10:4	10:5	10:6	10:7	10:8	10:9	10:10	10:11	11:0	11:1	11:2	11:3	

SCORE 70- IN THIS AREA

Conversion table: raw score (left/right) to standardised score by age (years:months).

Raw	11:3	11:2	11:1	11:0	10:11	10:10	10:9	10:8	10:7	10:6	10:5	10:4	10:3	10:2	10:1	10:0	9:11	9:10	9:9	9:8	9:7	9:6
76	80	80	80	81	81	81	82	82	82	83	83	83	84	84	84	85	85	86	86	87	87	88
77	80	80	81	81	81	82	82	82	83	83	83	84	84	84	85	85	86	86	86	87	88	88
78	80	81	81	81	81	82	82	82	83	83	84	84	84	85	85	86	86	87	87	87	88	89
79	81	81	81	82	82	82	82	83	83	84	84	84	85	85	86	86	86	87	87	88	89	89
80	81	81	81	82	82	82	83	83	84	84	84	85	85	85	86	86	87	87	87	88	89	90
81	81	81	82	82	82	83	83	83	84	84	85	85	85	86	86	87	87	88	88	89	90	90
82	81	82	82	82	82	83	83	84	84	85	85	85	86	86	87	87	88	88	88	89	90	91
83	82	82	82	83	83	83	84	84	84	85	85	86	86	87	87	87	88	89	89	90	91	91
84	82	82	83	83	83	83	84	84	85	85	86	86	86	87	87	88	88	89	89	90	91	92
85	82	83	83	83	83	84	84	85	85	86	86	86	87	87	88	88	89	90	90	91	92	93
86	83	83	83	83	84	84	85	85	85	86	86	87	87	88	88	89	89	90	90	91	92	93
87	83	83	83	84	84	84	85	85	86	86	87	87	87	88	89	89	90	90	91	92	93	94
88	83	83	84	84	84	85	85	86	86	87	87	87	88	89	89	90	90	91	91	92	94	95
89	83	84	84	84	85	85	86	86	86	87	87	88	88	89	90	90	91	92	92	93	95	96
90	84	84	84	85	85	85	86	86	87	88	88	88	89	89	90	91	92	92	93	94	95	96
91	84	84	85	85	85	86	86	87	87	88	88	89	89	90	91	91	92	92	93	94	96	97
92	84	85	85	85	86	86	87	87	87	88	89	89	90	91	91	92	93	93	94	95	97	98
93	85	85	85	86	86	86	87	87	88	89	89	90	90	91	92	93	94	94	95	96	98	99
94	85	85	86	86	86	87	88	88	88	89	90	90	91	92	93	93	94	95	96	97	99	100
95	85	86	86	87	87	87	88	88	89	90	90	91	92	92	93	94	95	95	96	98	100	101
96	85	86	86	87	87	88	88	89	89	90	91	91	92	93	94	95	96	96	97	98	101	102
97	86	86	87	87	87	88	89	89	90	91	91	92	93	94	95	96	97	97	98	99	102	103
98	86	86	87	87	88	88	89	89	90	91	92	93	94	94	95	97	98	98	99	100	103	104
99	86	87	87	88	88	89	89	90	91	92	92	93	94	95	96	97	99	99	100	101	104	105
100	87	87	88	88	89	89	90	90	91	92	93	94	95	96	97	98	100	100	101	102	105	107
101	87	87	88	89	89	90	90	91	92	93	94	95	96	97	98	99	101	101	102	103	106	108
102	87	88	88	89	90	90	91	91	93	94	95	96	97	98	99	100	102	102	103	105	108	109
103	88	88	89	89	90	91	92	92	93	94	95	96	98	99	100	101	103	103	104	106	109	111
104	88	89	89	90	91	91	92	92	94	95	96	97	99	100	101	103	104	104	106	107	111	112
105	89	89	90	91	91	92	93	93	95	96	97	98	100	101	102	104	105	106	107	109	112	114
106	89	90	90	91	92	93	94	94	96	97	98	99	101	102	103	105	107	107	109	111	114	115
107	90	90	91	92	93	93	94	95	97	98	99	100	102	103	105	107	108	109	111	112	115	116
108	90	90	91	92	93	94	95	95	98	99	100	102	103	105	106	108	110	110	112	114	116	118
109	91	91	92	93	94	95	96	96	99	100	101	103	104	106	108	110	112	112	114	115	118	120
110	91	91	92	94	95	96	97	97	100	101	102	104	106	108	110	112	114	114	115	116	120	122
111	92	92	93	94	96	97	98	98	101	102	104	106	107	110	112	113	115	115	116	118	122	124
112	92	93	94	95	96	98	99	99	102	103	105	107	109	112	113	115	116	116	118	120	124	126
113	93	93	94	96	97	99	100	100	103	105	107	109	112	113	115	117	119	119	121	122	127	129
114	94	94	95	97	99	100	101	102	105	107	109	111	113	115	117	119	121	121	123	125	130	
5 errors	95	96	97	98	100	101	103	104	107	109	111	113	115	117	119	122	124	127	129			
4 errors	95	97	98	99	101	102	104	106	109	111	113	115	117	120	122	125	128	130				
3 errors	96	98	99	100	102	104	106	108	111	113	115	118	120	123	126	129						
2 errors	97	98	100	102	103	106	108	111	113	115	118	121	124	128								
1 error	98	100	102	103	105	108	111	113	115	118	122	125	129									
no errors	100	101	103	105	107	110	113	115	119	122	127											

SCORE 130+ IN THIS AREA

Note: pupils scoring full marks and making no errors are at the ceiling of the test, so have *at least* the standardised score shown: their 'true' standardised score may be considerably higher.

27

TABLE B: Standardised scores for reading accuracy (for older, less able readers)

Note: There is a very strong ceiling effect in the test – over 2000 of the 9200 pupils read all the words correctly. Most of these were the older pupils. However, for those who did not achieve complete success, this table shows the SS scores: all are below the SS (mean) score of 100.

Age in years and completed months (with "SCORE 70- IN THIS AREA" occupying the blank upper-right cells)

6th error word	11:4	11:5	11:6	11:7	11:8	11:9	11:10	11:11	12:0	12:1	12:2	12:3	12:4	12:5	12:6	12:7	12:8	12:9	12:10	12:11	13:0	6th error word
40	70																					40
41	70	70																				41
42	70	70	70																			42
43	70	70	70	70																		43
44	71	71	70	70	70	70	70	70	70													44
45	71	71	71	70	70	70	70	70	70	70	70	70	70									45
46	71	71	71	70	70	70	70	70	70	70	70	70	70	70	70	70						46
47	71	71	71	71	70	70	70	70	70	70	70	70	70	70	70	70	70	70	70			47
48	72	72	71	71	71	71	70	71	70	70	70	70	70	70	70	70	70	70	70	70	70	48
49	72	72	72	71	71	71	71	71	71	70	70	70	70	70	70	70	70	70	70	70	70	49
50	72	72	72	71	71	71	71	71	71	71	70	70	70	70	70	70	70	70	70	70	70	50
51	72	72	72	71	71	71	71	71	71	71	71	71	71	71	71	71	70	70	70	70	70	51
52	73	73	72	72	72	72	71	72	71	71	71	71	71	71	71	71	71	71	70	70	70	52
53	73	73	73	72	72	72	72	72	71	71	71	71	71	71	71	71	71	71	71	71	70	53
54	73	73	73	73	72	72	72	72	72	72	71	71	71	71	71	71	71	71	71	71	71	54
55	74	73	73	73	72	72	72	72	72	72	72	71	71	71	71	71	71	71	71	71	71	55
56	74	74	73	73	73	73	72	73	72	72	72	72	72	72	72	72	72	71	71	71	71	56
57	74	74	74	73	73	73	73	73	72	72	72	72	72	72	72	72	72	72	71	71	71	57
58	74	74	74	73	73	73	73	73	72	72	73	72	72	72	72	72	72	72	72	72	71	58
59	75	74	74	73	73	73	73	73	73	73	73	72	72	73	72	72	72	72	72	72	72	59
60	75	75	74	74	74	74	73	74	73	73	73	73	73	73	73	73	73	73	73	72	72	60
61	75	75	75	74	74	74	74	74	73	73	73	73	73	73	73	73	73	73	73	73	72	61
62	75	75	75	75	74	74	74	74	73	73	73	73	73	73	73	73	73	73	73	73	72	62
63	76	75	75	75	74	74	74	74	73	73	73	73	73	73	73	73	73	73	73	73	72	63
64	76	76	75	75	75	75	74	75	74	74	74	74	73	74	74	74	74	74	73	73	73	64
65	76	76	76	75	75	75	75	75	74	74	74	74	74	74	74	74	74	74	74	73	73	65
66	76	76	76	76	75	75	75	75	74	74	74	74	74	74	74	74	74	74	74	74	73	66
67	77	77	76	76	75	75	75	75	74	75	74	74	74	74	74	74	74	74	74	74	73	67
68	77	77	77	76	76	76	76	76	74	75	75	75	74	75	75	74	75	75	74	74	73	68
69	77	77	77	76	76	76	76	76	75	75	75	75	75	75	75	75	75	75	75	75	74	69
70	78	77	77	77	76	76	76	76	75	75	75	75	75	75	75	75	75	75	75	75	74	70
71	78	78	77	77	77	76	76	76	75	76	76	75	75	75	75	75	75	75	75	75	74	71
72	78	78	78	77	77	77	76	77	76	76	76	76	75	76	76	76	75	75	75	75	74	72
73	78	78	78	77	77	77	77	77	76	76	76	76	76	76	76	76	76	76	75	75	75	73
74	79	79	78	78	77	77	77	77	76	77	77	76	76	76	76	76	76	76	76	76	75	74
75	79	79	78	78	78	77	77	77	77	77	77	77	77	77	76	76	76	76	76	76	75	75
76	79	79	79	78	78	78	78	78	77	77	77	77	77	77	76	76	76	76	76	76	75	76
77	80	79	79	79	78	78	78	78	77	77	77	77	77	77	76	76	76	76	76	75	75	77
78	80	80	79	79	79	78	78	78	78	78	78	77	77	77	77	76	76	76	76	76	75	78
79	80	80	80	79	79	79	79	78	78	78	78	77	77	77	77	77	76	76	76	76	76	79
6th error word	11:4	11:5	11:6	11:7	11:8	11:9	11:10	11:11	12:0	12:1	12:2	12:3	12:4	12:5	12:6	12:7	12:8	12:9	12:10	12:11	13:0	6th error word

	11:4	11:5	11:6	11:7	11:8	11:9	11:10	11:11	12:0	12:1	12:2	12:3	12:4	12:5	12:6	12:7	12:8	12:9	12:10	12:11	13:0	
80	81	80	80	80	79	79	79	79	78	78	78	78	77	77	77	77	77	76	76	76	76	80
81	81	81	80	80	80	79	79	79	79	78	78	78	78	77	77	77	77	77	76	76	76	81
82	81	81	80	80	80	79	79	79	79	79	78	78	78	78	77	77	77	77	77	76	76	82
83	81	81	81	80	80	80	79	79	79	79	78	78	78	78	78	77	77	77	77	77	76	83
84	82	82	81	81	80	80	80	79	79	79	79	79	79	78	78	78	77	77	77	77	77	84
85	82	82	81	81	81	80	80	80	80	79	79	79	79	78	78	78	78	78	77	77	77	85
86	82	82	82	81	81	80	80	80	80	79	79	79	79	79	78	78	78	78	78	77	77	86
87	82	82	82	81	81	81	80	80	80	80	80	79	79	79	79	78	78	78	78	78	77	87
88	83	82	82	82	81	81	81	80	80	80	80	80	80	79	79	79	78	78	78	78	78	88
89	83	83	82	82	82	81	81	81	81	80	80	80	80	79	79	79	79	78	78	78	78	89
90	83	83	83	82	82	82	81	81	81	81	80	80	80	80	79	79	79	79	78	78	78	90
91	84	83	83	83	82	82	81	81	81	81	81	80	80	80	80	79	79	79	79	78	78	91
92	84	84	83	83	83	82	82	82	81	81	81	81	81	80	80	80	79	79	79	79	78	92
93	84	84	84	83	83	82	82	82	82	81	81	81	81	80	80	80	80	79	79	79	79	93
94	84	84	84	83	83	83	82	82	82	82	81	81	81	81	80	80	80	80	79	79	79	94
95	85	84	84	84	83	83	83	83	82	82	82	81	81	81	81	80	80	80	80	79	79	95
96	85	85	84	84	83	83	83	83	82	82	82	82	82	81	81	81	80	80	80	79	79	96
97	85	85	85	84	84	83	83	83	83	82	82	82	82	81	81	81	81	80	80	80	80	97
98	86	85	85	85	84	84	83	83	83	83	82	82	82	82	81	81	81	81	80	80	80	98
99	86	86	85	85	84	84	84	84	83	83	83	82	82	82	82	81	81	81	81	80	80	99
100	86	86	86	85	85	84	84	84	84	83	83	83	82	82	82	82	81	81	81	80	80	100
101	87	86	86	85	85	85	84	84	84	83	83	83	83	82	82	82	82	81	81	81	81	101
102	87	87	86	86	85	85	85	84	84	84	83	83	83	83	82	82	82	82	81	81	81	102
103	87	87	86	86	86	85	85	85	84	84	84	83	83	83	83	82	82	82	81	81	81	103
104	88	87	87	86	86	86	85	85	85	84	84	84	83	83	83	83	82	82	82	81	81	104
105	88	88	87	87	86	86	86	85	85	84	84	84	84	83	83	83	83	82	82	82	81	105
106	89	88	87	87	87	86	86	85	85	85	84	84	84	84	83	83	83	82	82	82	82	106
107	89	88	88	87	87	87	86	86	85	85	85	84	84	84	84	83	83	83	82	82	82	107
108	89	89	88	88	87	87	86	86	86	85	85	85	84	84	84	84	83	83	83	82	82	108
109	90	89	89	88	88	87	87	86	86	86	85	85	85	84	84	84	84	83	83	83	82	109
110	90	90	89	89	88	88	87	87	86	86	86	85	85	85	84	84	84	83	83	83	83	110
111	91	90	90	89	88	88	87	87	87	86	86	86	85	85	84	84	84	84	83	83	83	111
112	92	91	90	90	89	88	88	87	87	87	86	86	85	85	85	85	84	84	84	83	83	112
113	92	91	91	90	89	89	88	88	87	87	87	87	86	85	85	85	85	84	84	84	83	113
114	93	92	91	90	90	89	89	88	88	87	87	87	86	86	85	85	85	84	84	84	84	114
5 errors	94	93	92	91	90	90	89	89	88	87	87	87	86	86	86	85	85	85	84	84	84	5 errors
4 errors	94	93	92	92	91	90	89	89	88	88	87	87	87	86	86	86	85	85	85	84	84	4 errors
3 errors	95	94	93	92	91	91	90	89	88	88	87	87	87	86	86	86	85	85	85	84	84	3 errors
2 errors	96	95	94	93	92	91	90	90	89	89	88	88	87	87	86	86	86	85	85	85	84	2 errors
1 error	97	96	95	94	93	92	91	90	90	89	89	88	88	87	87	86	86	86	85	85	85	1 error
	11:4	11:5	11:6	11:7	11:8	11:9	11:10	11:11	12:0	12:1	12:2	12:3	12:4	12:5	12:6	12:7	12:8	12:9	12:10	12:11	13:0	

TABLE C: Standardised scores for comprehension

Age in years and completed months

Raw score	7:6	7:5	7:4	7:3	7:2	7:1	7:0	6:11	6:10	6:9	6:8	6:7	6:6	6:5	6:4	6:3	6:2	6:1	6:0	5:11	5:10	Raw score
1																						1
2																				70	71	2
3														70	71	72	74	75	76	77	78	3
4							70	70	71	72	73	74	75	76	77	77	78	79	80	81	82	4
5	70	70	71	72	72	73	74	75	75	76	77	78	78	79	80	81	82	83	83	84	85	5
6	73	74	74	75	76	76	77	78	79	79	80	81	82	82	83	84	85	85	86	87	87	6
7	76	77	77	78	79	79	80	81	82	82	83	84	84	85	86	86	87	88	89	89	90	7
8	79	80	80	81	81	82	83	83	84	85	85	86	87	87	88	89	90	90	91	92	93	8
9	81	82	83	83	84	84	85	86	86	87	88	88	89	90	91	91	92	93	93	94	94	9
10	84	84	85	85	86	87	87	88	89	89	90	91	92	92	93	94	94	95	95	96	97	10
11	86	87	87	88	88	89	90	91	91	92	93	93	94	94	95	96	96	97	98	99	100	11
12	88	89	89	90	91	92	92	93	93	94	95	95	96	97	98	98	99	100	101	101	102	12
13	90	91	92	93	93	94	94	95	96	96	97	98	99	100	100	101	102	102	103	104	105	13
14	93	93	94	95	95	96	97	98	98	99	100	101	101	102	103	104	105	105	106	106	107	14
15	95	96	96	97	98	99	100	100	101	102	103	104	104	105	106	106	107	107	108	109	109	15
16	98	99	99	100	101	102	102	103	104	105	106	106	107	107	108	108	109	110	111	111	112	16
17	101	101	102	103	104	105	105	106	107	107	108	108	109	110	111	111	112	113	113	114	114	17
18	104	104	105	106	107	107	108	108	109	110	111	111	112	113	114	114	115	115	116	116	117	18
19	106	107	108	108	109	110	111	112	112	113	114	114	115	115	116	117	117	118	119	119	120	19
20	109	110	111	112	112	113	114	114	115	115	116	117	118	118	119	120	120	121	121	122	123	20
21	112	113	114	114	115	116	116	117	118	119	119	120	121	121	122	123	123	124	124	125	126	21
22	115	116	117	117	118	119	120	120	121	122	122	123	124	124	125	126	126	127	128	128	129	22
23	119	119	120	121	122	122	123	124	124	125	126	126	127	128	128	129	130	130				23
24	122	123	124	124	125	126	127	127	128	129	129	130										24
25	126	127	127	128	129	130	130															25
26	130																					26
27																						27
28														SCORE 130+ IN THIS AREA								28
29																						29
30																						30
31																						31
32																						32
33																						33
34																						34
	7:6	7:5	7:4	7:3	7:2	7:1	7:0	6:11	6:10	6:9	6:8	6:7	6:6	6:5	6:4	6:3	6:2	6:1	6:0	5:11	5:10	

Age in years and completed months

Age in years and completed months

Raw score	7:7	7:8	7:9	7:10	7:11	8:0	8:1	8:2	8:3	8:4	8:5	8:6	8:7	8:8	8:9	8:10	8:11	9:0	9:1	9:2	9:3
1																					
2																					
3																					
4																					
5																					
6	73	72	71	71	71	70	70														
7	76	75	74	74	73	73	72	72	71	71	71	70	70								
8	78	78	77	76	76	75	75	74	74	73	73	72	72	72	71	71	71	70	70	70	
9	81	80	80	79	78	78	77	77	76	76	75	75	74	74	73	73	73	72	72	72	71
10	83	82	82	81	81	80	80	79	78	78	77	77	76	76	76	75	75	74	74	73	73
11	85	85	84	83	83	82	82	81	81	80	80	79	79	78	78	77	77	76	76	75	75
12	88	87	86	86	85	84	84	83	83	82	82	81	81	80	80	79	79	78	78	77	77
13	90	89	88	88	87	87	86	85	85	84	84	83	83	82	82	81	81	80	80	79	79
14	92	92	91	90	89	89	88	88	87	86	86	85	84	84	83	83	82	82	81	81	81
15	94	94	93	93	92	91	90	90	89	88	88	87	87	86	85	85	84	84	83	83	82
16	97	96	95	95	94	93	93	92	92	91	90	89	89	88	88	87	86	86	85	85	84
17	100	99	98	97	96	96	95	94	94	93	93	92	91	90	90	89	88	88	87	87	86
18	103	102	101	100	99	99	98	97	96	95	94	94	93	93	92	91	91	90	89	89	88
19	106	105	104	103	102	101	101	100	99	98	97	96	96	95	94	94	93	92	92	91	90
20	108	107	107	106	106	105	104	103	102	101	100	99	99	98	97	96	95	94	94	93	93
21	112	111	110	109	108	107	107	106	105	104	103	102	102	101	100	99	98	97	96	96	95
22	114	114	113	113	112	111	110	109	108	107	107	106	105	104	103	102	101	100	100	99	98
23	118	117	116	115	115	114	113	113	112	111	110	109	108	107	106	106	105	104	103	102	101
24	121	121	120	119	118	117	116	115	115	114	113	113	112	110	109	108	108	107	106	105	104
25	125	124	124	123	122	121	120	119	119	118	117	116	115	114	113	113	112	110	109	108	107
26	129	129	128	127	126	125	124	123	123	122	121	120	119	118	117	116	115	114	114	113	112
27						130	129	128	127	126	125	124	123	122	122	121	120	119	117	116	115
28											130	129	128	127	126	125	124	123	122	121	120
29																	130	129	128	127	125
30																					
31																					
32																					
33																					
34																					

SCORE 70- IN THIS AREA

SCORE 130+ IN THIS AREA

Age in years and completed months

TABLE C cont

Age in years and completed months

Raw score	9:4	9:5	9:6	9:7	9:8	9:9	9:10	9:11	10:0	10:1	10:2	10:3	10:4	10:5	10:6	10:7	10:8	10:9	10:10	10:11	11:0	Raw score
1																						1
2																						2
3																						3
4																						4
5																						5
6																						6
7																						7
8																						8
9	71	71	70	70	70	70																9
10	73	72	72	72	71	71	71	71	70	70	70	70										10
11	75	74	74	73	73	73	73	72	72	72	71	71	71	71	70	70	70	70	70			11
12	76	76	76	75	75	75	74	74	74	73	73	73	72	72	72	72	71	71	71	71	70	12
13	78	78	77	77	77	76	76	75	75	75	74	74	74	74	73	73	73	72	72	72	72	13
14	80	80	79	79	78	78	78	77	77	76	76	76	75	75	75	74	74	74	74	73	73	14
15	82	81	81	81	80	80	79	79	78	78	78	77	77	77	76	76	76	75	75	75	74	15
16	84	83	83	82	82	81	81	80	80	80	79	79	78	78	78	77	77	77	76	76	76	16
17	85	85	84	84	83	83	83	82	82	81	81	80	80	80	79	79	79	78	78	78	77	17
18	88	87	86	86	85	85	84	84	83	83	82	82	82	81	81	80	80	80	79	79	79	18
19	90	89	88	88	87	87	86	86	85	84	84	84	83	83	82	82	82	81	81	80	80	19
20	92	91	91	90	89	89	88	88	87	86	86	85	85	84	84	83	83	83	82	82	81	20
21	94	93	93	92	92	91	90	90	89	88	88	87	87	86	86	85	85	84	84	83	83	21
22	97	96	95	94	94	93	93	92	91	91	90	89	89	88	88	87	86	86	85	85	84	22
23	100	99	98	97	96	95	95	94	93	93	92	92	91	90	89	89	88	88	87	87	86	23
24	103	102	101	101	100	99	98	97	96	95	94	94	93	93	92	91	90	90	89	89	88	24
25	107	106	105	104	103	102	101	100	99	98	97	96	95	95	94	93	93	92	92	91	90	25
26	110	109	108	107	107	106	105	104	103	101	101	100	99	98	97	96	95	94	94	93	93	26
27	114	114	113	112	110	109	108	107	106	106	104	103	102	101	100	99	98	97	96	95	95	27
28	119	118	117	116	115	114	113	112	110	109	108	107	106	105	104	103	102	101	100	99	98	28
29	124	123	122	121	120	119	117	116	115	114	113	112	110	109	108	107	106	105	104	102	101	29
30	130	129	128	127	125	124	123	122	121	119	118	116	115	114	113	112	110	109	108	107	106	30
31							130	129	127	126	124	123	121	120	119	117	115	114	113	112	110	31
32													129	128	126	124	123	121	119	118	116	32
33																		130	128	126	124	33
34																						34
	9:4	9:5	9:6	9:7	9:8	9:9	9:10	9:11	10:0	10:1	10:2	10:3	10:4	10:5	10:6	10:7	10:8	10:9	10:10	10:11	11:0	

SCORE 70- IN THIS AREA (upper blank region)

SCORE 130+ IN THIS AREA (lower blank region)

Age in years and completed months

Age in years and completed months

Raw score	11:1	11:2	11:3	11:4	11:5	11:6	11:7	11:8	11:9	11:10	11:11	12:0	12:1	12:2	12:3	12:4	12:5	12:6	12:7	Raw score
1																				1
2																				2
3																				3
4																				4
5																				5
6																				6
7																				7
8																				8
9																				9
10																				10
11																				11
12	70	70	70	70	70															12
13	72	71	71	71	71	70	70	70	70	70	70									13
14	73	73	72	72	72	72	71	71	71	71	71	70	70	70	70	70	70			14
15	74	74	74	73	73	73	73	72	72	72	72	72	71	71	71	71	71	71	70	15
16	75	75	75	75	74	74	74	74	73	73	73	73	73	72	72	72	72	72	71	16
17	77	77	76	76	76	75	75	75	75	74	74	74	74	73	73	73	73	73	72	17
18	78	78	78	77	77	77	76	76	76	76	75	75	75	75	74	74	74	74	73	18
19	80	79	79	79	78	78	78	77	77	77	77	76	76	76	75	75	75	75	74	19
20	81	81	80	80	80	79	79	79	78	78	78	77	77	77	77	76	76	76	76	20
21	83	82	82	81	81	81	80	80	80	79	79	79	78	78	78	78	77	77	77	21
22	84	84	83	83	82	82	82	81	81	81	80	80	80	79	79	79	79	78	78	22
23	86	85	85	84	84	83	83	83	82	82	82	81	81	81	80	80	80	79	79	23
24	88	87	86	86	85	85	85	84	84	83	83	83	82	82	82	81	81	81	80	24
25	89	89	88	88	87	87	86	86	85	85	84	84	84	83	83	83	82	82	82	25
26	92	91	90	90	89	89	88	88	87	87	86	86	85	85	84	84	84	83	83	26
27	94	93	93	92	91	91	90	89	89	88	88	87	87	86	86	85	85	84	84	27
28	97	96	95	94	94	93	92	92	91	90	90	89	89	88	88	87	87	86	86	28
29	100	99	98	97	96	95	94	94	93	93	92	91	91	90	89	89	88	88	87	29
30	105	103	102	101	100	99	98	97	96	95	94	94	93	92	92	91	90	90	89	30
31	109	107	106	105	104	103	101	100	99	98	97	96	95	94	94	93	93	92	91	31
32	115	113	112	110	108	107	106	105	104	102	101	100	99	98	97	96	95	94	93	32
33	122	120	118	117	115	113	112	110	108	107	106	105	103	102	101	99	98	97	96	33
34			129	127	124	122	120	117	115	114	112	110	108	107	106	104	103	101	100	34
	11:1	11:2	11:3	11:4	11:5	11:6	11:7	11:8	11:9	11:10	11:11	12:0	12:1	12:2	12:3	12:4	12:5	12:6	12:7	

SCORE 70- IN THIS AREA

Age in years and completed months

Note: pupils scoring full marks are at the ceiling of the test, so have *at least* the standardised score shown: their 'true' standardised score may be considerably higher.

TABLE D: Standardised scores for comprehension (for older, less able readers)

Note: because many of the 9200 pupils did well with the comprehension questions, getting at least 30 correct, the SS table indicates the norm for complete success is 12:7 years. This table gives standardised scores for those pupils who are older and not totally successful: all are below the SS (mean) score of 100.

Age in years and completed months

Raw score	12:8	12:9	12:10	12:11	13:0	13:1	13:2	13:3	13:4	13:5	13:6	13:7	13:8	13:9	13:10	13:11	14:0	Raw score
10																		10
11																		11
12																		12
13																		13
14																		14
15	70	70	70															15
16	71	71	71	70	70	70	70	70	70	70	70							16
17	72	72	72	71	71	71	71	71	71	71	71	70	70	70	70	70	70	17
18	73	73	73	72	72	72	72	72	72	72	71	71	71	71	71	71	71	18
19	74	74	74	73	72	73	73	73	73	73	72	72	72	72	72	72	71	19
20	75	75	75	74	73	74	74	74	74	74	73	73	73	73	73	72	72	20
21	76	76	76	75	74	75	75	75	75	74	74	74	74	74	74	73	73	21
22	78	77	77	76	75	76	76	76	76	75	75	75	75	75	74	74	74	22
23	79	79	78	77	77	77	77	77	77	76	76	76	76	76	75	75	75	23
24	80	80	79	78	78	79	78	78	78	78	77	77	77	77	76	76	76	24
25	81	81	81	79	79	80	79	79	79	79	78	78	78	78	77	77	77	25
26	82	82	82	80	80	81	81	80	80	80	79	79	79	79	78	78	78	26
27	84	83	83	82	81	82	82	81	81	81	81	80	80	80	79	79	79	27
28	85	85	84	84	82	83	83	83	82	82	82	81	81	81	81	80	80	28
29	87	86	86	85	84	85	84	84	84	83	83	83	82	82	82	81	81	29
30	89	88	88	87	85	86	86	85	85	84	84	84	83	83	83	83	82	30
31	91	90	89	89	87	88	87	87	86	86	85	85	85	84	84	84	83	31
32	93	92	92	91	90	90	89	89	88	88	87	87	86	86	85	85	84	32
33	95	94	94	93	93	92	91	90	90	89	89	88	88	87	87	86	86	33
Raw score	12:8	12:9	12:10	12:11	13:0	13:1	13:2	13:3	13:4	13:5	13:6	13:7	13:8	13:9	13:10	13:11	14:0	Raw score

SCORE 70- IN THIS AREA

Age in years and completed months

SCHOOLS WHICH SUPPLIED DATA FOR THE REVISION AND RESTANDARDISATION

We wish to thank all of the pupils and staff in the following schools, which were involved in the trialling.

Abbotswood Junior School, Totton, SO40 8EB

Acton High School, London, W3 8EY

Alfriston School, Beaconsfield, HP9 2TS

Ambler Primary School, Islington, N4 2DR

Applemore College, Dibden Purlieu, SO45 4RQ

Broad Chalke Primary School, Broad Chalke, SP5 5DS

Brooklands Primary School, Brantham, CO11 1RX

Bryn Celynnog Comprehensive School, Beddau, CF38 2AE

Carleton Park Junior and Infants School, Carleton, WF8 3PT

Catton Grove Primary School, Norwich, NR3 3TP

Cirencester Primary School, Cirencester, GL7 1EX

Dinas Powys Infants School, Cogan, CF64 4JU

Elson Junior School, Gosport, PO12 4EX

Epworth Primary School, Epworth, DN9 1DL

Exning Primary School, Exning, CB8 7EW

Fred Nicholson Special School, Dereham, NR19 1JB

Front Lawn Junior School, Leigh Park, PO9 5HX

Galliard Primary School, Enfield, N9 7PE

Gooseacre Primary School, Rotherham, S63 0NU

Grange Primary School, Felixstowe, IP11 2LA

Greendown School, Swindon, SN5 6HN

Greenhill Primary School, Gelligaer, CF82 8EU

Groggan Primary School, Randalstown, BT41 3EU

Guilsfield Primary School, Welshpool, SY21 9ND

Hethersett High School, Hethersett, NR9 3DB

Killeen Primary School, Newry, BT35 8RX

La Mare de Carteret Primary School, Castel, GY57FL

Leys Farm Junior School, Bottesford, DN17 2PB

Little Hallingbury C of E Primary School, Little Hallingbury, CM22 7RE

Long Buckby Infants and Junior School, Long Buckby, NN6 7RE

Machynlleth Primary School, Machynlleth, SY20 8HE

Manland Primary School, Harpenden, AL5 4QW

Manor Fields Primary School, Salisbury, SP2 7EJ

Newlands Spring Primary School, Chelmsford, CM1 4UU

Notley Green Primary School, Great Notley, CM77 7ZJ.

Oakfield Primary School, Barry, CF62 9DU

Our Lady and St John Catholic College, Blackburn, BB1 1PY

Oxley Park Primary School, Oxley Park, MK4 4TA

Pleckgate High School, Blackburn, BB1 8QA

Scaltback Middle School, Newmarket, CB8 0DJ

Sheringham Primary School, Manor Park, E12 5PB

Sponne School, Towcester, NN12 6DJ

St Andrew's C of E Primary School, Headington, OX3 9ED

St Andrew's C of E Primary School, Weeley, CO16 9DH

St John the Baptist C of E Primary School, Royston, S71 4QY

St John's C of E Primary School, Rownhams, SO16 8AD

St Kevin's Community School, Dublin 8

St Luke's C of E Primary School, Tiptree, CO5 0SU

St Martin at Shouldham C of E Primary School, Shouldham, PE33 0BU

St Martin's C of E Primary School, Owston Ferry, DN9 1AY

St Mary's Primary School, Maghera, BT46 5AP

St Michael's C of E Primary School, Figheldean, SP4 8JT

St Nicholas C of E Primary School, Ulceby, DN39 6TB

St Peter's C of E Primary School, Tankersley, S75 3DA

Stisted C of E Primary School, Stisted, CM77 8AN

Sulhamstead and Ufton Nervet Primary School, Ufton Nervet, RG7 4 HQ

Summerfield Primary School, Bradwell Common, MK13 8PG

Swaythling Primary School, Swathling, SO17 3SZ

Sythwood Primary School, Sythwood, GU21 3AX

The Bliss School, Nether Heyford, NN7 3LE

Thompson Primary School, Thompson, IP24 1PY

Thornhill Primary School, Hackney, N1 1HX

Tuddenham C of E Primary School, Tuddenham St Mary, IP28 6SA

Tylers Green Middle School, Tylers Green, HP10 8DS

West Drayton Primary School, West Drayton, UB7 9EA

Westwoodside C of E Primary School, Westwoodside, DN9 2DR

Wetherby High School, Wetherby, LS22 6JS

White Notley C of E Primary School, White Notely, CM8 1RZ

Wimborne Infants School, Southsea, PO4 0LS

Windermere Primary School, St Albans, AL1 5QP

Woodstock Primary School, Woodstock, OX20 1LL

Wakefield Learning Support Team, Wakefield, WF1 4RJ

READING FOR MEANING
interpretation graph

Pupil's name: ....

Use a different colour to record and plot each test date:

Form A: ....

Form B: ....

Form C: ....

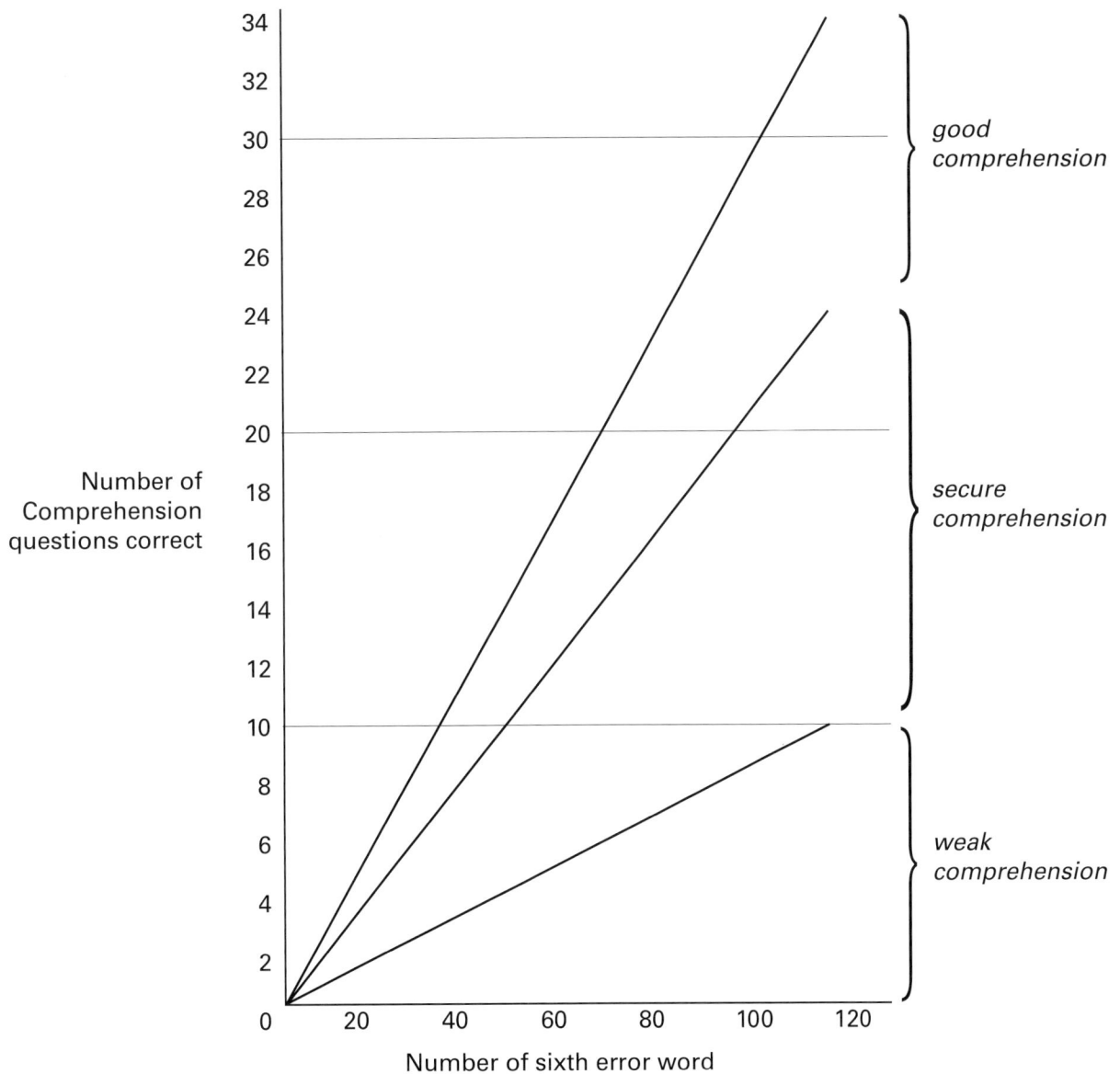

New Salford Sentence Reading Test: photocopy master